For most of my life I ha
We have a sense that we
from a different cloth th

somehow seem to gracel. , ____ around in social settings- fitting in perfectly, while we are awkwardly apprehensive in the corner wondering why we came in the first place. We all know the feeling. The Outcast. Many of our predecessors knew this label well, too.

The Witches from the old days had it bad. For starters… We are spoiled by modern technology. I am the first to admit that I sometimes feel as if I could not live without electricity and social media. I *know* that I could, but it would really suck. In the Old Days, they had to kill their food if they planned on eating. We can run to Walmart and pick up something to throw in the microwave and have a ready cooked meal in less than three minutes. They spent countless hours planning for meals. All their time was pretty much spent focusing on Survival. They *struggled* to survive in those days. If it was not starvation, it was some plague, beast or force of nature that done them in. They struggled to Survive. We simply exist. Usually spending our time trying to fill the void that all this technology leaves by making our lives too easy.

I am not complaining. I am simply stating that so many of us take for granted the luxuries that we are so accustomed to. Our Ancestors would be baffled. They honestly would not know what to do with themselves.

So aside from struggling every minute of every day, the Witches of Old were feared, hated, socially rejected and manipulated. They were used and abused and inevitably destroyed in one form or another. If they didn't get executed for their so-called crimes against the Church, they were treated as pariahs. Shunned and set apart from everyone they knew. They could not go borrow a cup of milk from the neighbor to feed their starving baby. Hell, Witches were lucky that a crazed mob didn't burn down their house and steal their livestock. So, with these things being said, please take a moment and try to realize how incredibly lucky you are to be a Modern Witch. Understand that you are truly blessed to have an easier life than our ancestors had. Witches may not have *exactly easy* these days, but they damn sure have it better than they would have in 1692.

Sure... The Broom Closet can be uncomfortable, and a little cramped with all these 'Pop Culture' chasing witches hopping in there with us. But honestly, we have it rather good these days in the USA, where Wicca and other forms of Witchcraft are considered religions. In Many parts of Africa and Saudi Arabia you could be *KILLED* for walking our path. And you thought The Bible Belt was Bad! Ha, Not Hardly! I am amazed to say that I get more shit about my tattoos than I do for my Tarot Cards.

I Personally Want to Dedicate This Book to Several People. It's a bit of a list, so get comfortable.

Dedicated to:

The Goddess Hecate (My Personal Deity)

My Family- My Husband, Girls and Grandbabies

Chris, Haley, Maddie, Jax and Liam

My Parents and My Sister, Who I miss Terribly every Day

My Coven- AKA The Dirty Dozen

Eris, Azera, Thorn, Onix, Faeryn, Bryar, Corvis, Merlin, Reaper, Janus, Damien and All of our Seekers & Members

My Besties- Y'all know who tf you are

The Silver Moon Society

WonderLost Inkorpserrated

All of My Followers and Patrons from Facebook and Patreon

Teresa, my first Patron on Patreon

This book is intended to help anyone interested in walking the Path of The Witches. It will have some history, some basic knowledge about Witchcraft and Paganism, and plenty of Spells. Buckle Up, Witches!

Chapter 1

A Few Facts about the History of Witchery and Paganism

The mere word 'Witchcraft' conjures up all sorts of fantasies and stereotypes for much of the population. According to fictional literature and television, up until only pretty recent years, to be considered a Witch was an awful and terrifying thing. Awful, because Witches were supposedly the 'Devil's Handmaidens' or completely malicious beings who thrived on the suffering of the innocent and fed on the flesh of infants among many other horrendous, yet imaginary notions. The terrifying part came with the torture that was usually set about to extract a false confession of 'Satanism'.

The 'Malleus Maleficarum' was a book in written in 1487 by a Witch Hunter from Germany named Heinrich Kramer. He had been denied fulfilling his weird fantastical obsession with hurting innocent Women and breeding fear, so his publishing of this book was a seriously messed up, albeit pretty smart tactic to sway the public into a state of mass hysteria. The Roman Church FINALLY banned the book in 1490, but by then it was too late. He had spread his fear and mania all over Europe and to many other parts of the world by this point.

The Book, Which roughly translates to 'Hammer against Witches' or Hammer of Evil Doers basically was an instruction manual on how to supposedly identify Witches and how to use certain methods of physical restraint and torture to force them to confess to their suspected crimes against the church. In fact, the Hysteria had become so widely spread that even the Spanish Inquisition warned its own members not to believe everything that the book said, even if they thought they had secured substantial evidence in their cases against the accused. By the time 1520 rolled around, it had reprinted in 14 editions and became very influential in courtrooms because of its notoriety. Many Protestant Churches tried to justify their executions by claiming that Witches were involved in Orgiastic Satanic Ceremonies and Rites and that they cannibalized babies.

The first major Witchcraft Persecution in Europe that involved Accused Witches being caught, tried, convicted and burned to death at the stake is said to have occurred in Wiesensteig in Southwest Germany. It was written about in a pamphlet that was published in 1563 called 'True and Horrifying Deeds of 63 Witches'.

From 1644 until 1647 the maniacal reign of Matthew Hopkins, self-proclaimed Witch Finder General (Completely made up title, by the way) and his merry band of assholes would roam from town to town trying to sniff out Witches for riches. They would charge ridiculously high fees to rid them of their undesirables before moving on to the next. There were at least 300 convictions and deaths that he is responsible for.

Hopkins' methods were pretty heinous. To extract confessions, there were many ways he could hurt these victims. Usually first, they would be stripped down naked and completely humiliated (As these were Puritan Days) And Man-handled while searched for a 'Witches Mark'. This could be a mole, a freckle, birthmark or even a mild deformity. This is where they were thought to suckle their familiars, In addition to this, and literally add injury to insult- they would then have needles or pins stabbed into various parts of their bodies, usually near these 'Witch Marks', to see if they felt it, or if they'd bleed... because surely a witch is inhuman.

Now, this is where it goes really dark. If you are squeamish you may not want to read the rest of this post. This is where the conversation turns to the Horrendous shit. The other forms of torture that were employed.

Sleep Deprivation is the first one we will talk about. These poor souls would be kept awake for days. If they started to pass out from the exhaustion, they would be whipped or stood up and paced to keep them awake. When the Torturers felt they had enough, they interrogate them until they got their desired answer.

Rinse and Repeat.

Then there was the Cutting. They would literally slice them with knives to make them talk, turn over 'accomplices' or confess. Pincers would claw at and rip the flesh from the tired, beaten bodies as a similar technique. The Thumb Screws were like little tiny iron vices that were put on the fingers and toes and tightened until the bones snapped like twigs.

There was also Dunking or Swimming the Witch. This was a perversion of the Baptism. The accused would be dunked or thrown into deep water with no way of escaping. If she sank, she was innocent of Witchcraft. But she was also dead, If she floated, she was rejecting the Baptismal Waters and therefore an unholy creature, so then she'd be killed another way. Another Torture Technique was Pressing. This technique was used on Giles Corey in Salem who refused to give a false confession of witchcraft. He was put on the ground on his back and had large slabs of stone stacked on top of him, one at a time until he died.

Then there are these guys. The Witches Bridle, The Heretic's Fork and The Pear of Anguish. The Bridle was a little less brutal, in that it was a metal device placed over the face and partially over the head that had a metal fixture that went inside the mouth preventing talking. The Heretic's Fork was a contraption that was similar to a spike that was strapped to upright the front of their eyes. When she would blink, her eyelids would be pierced. Alternatively, it was strapped to the front of the neck, forcing the head into a backwards tilt, unable to tilt forward or long periods of time. Probably many days or more. The Pear of Anguish was not unlike the duckbill used for pap smears nowadays. Except it was huge, spiked and cranked open in any orifice resulting in probable rupture of internal cavities.

And Last but not least... we have the 'Ole Traditional Stake Burning. This was an especially evil way to kill someone. If the smoke inhalation did not do you in, the excruciatingly penetrating, searing pain was sure to give you a heart attack. If you were lucky you would have passed out unconscious from the pain early on, while the crowd of angry or curious onlookers gawked at your sizzling flesh.

All That Hatred. So damn sad. Most of the people that were accused of and executed for witchcraft were women. Usually widowed, elderly, poor or mentally handicapped. Sometimes just ornery old women or ladies that didn't take no shit from anyone. That is what those big, tough men were afraid of. The almighty *VAGINA* and the helpless woman attached to it. In actuality, I have my theories about that. It wasn't the poo-nanny itself that they feared. It was the toppling of the Patriarchy when the Wild Women rose to power, once again.

This book is for Anyone seeking arcane knowledge, or who wants to commune with Nature and learn the Magick of the Elements. The knowledge contained in these pages come from my Coven, The Silver Moon Society, based in Southeast Georgia. We do not follow a specific Deity. We are an eclectic Coven, meaning that we draw from many paths to forge our own. In our Coven, we each worship our own Deities and abide by our own individual preferences in the way we worship. We all follow the Wiccan Rede, as a set of Basic guidelines. We meet the third Saturday of each month, on for the Eight Sabbats of the Wheel of The Year. Our Elders, and sometimes the entire Coven meets every full moon and new moon as well. We accept anyone who approaches us, within reason. We do not tolerate illicit drug use, alcoholism, illegal activities or drama in our Circles. We all check our Baggage at the Door when we meet up.

We host a Podcast and have a Patreon and are currently working on a You Tube and Vimeo Channel. I personally, also have a Webstore that specializes in Pagan Supplies. We have a Facebook Page called The Silver Moon Society- HEX Appeal, and my personal page is HEX Appeal with Raven Nightshade. Feel free to check us out! We are always open to new seekers and initiates. I am also currently working on putting together a Pagan Charitable Organization. My goal is to be an Outreach Program for the Families and Individuals who do not feel comfortable accepting Charity from a religion who sees them as Evil or False, or otherwise does not have anyone to turn to in times of need. We will help anyone who needs it within our capabilities, regardless of their religious preference or lifestyle. But I especially want to state that I am doing this because times are hard for everyone, but I *KNOW* what it is like to be a Pagan in need and feel like a piece of shit- asking for help from a Christian Church when they fear and do not understand our Path. I know the struggle, and I do not like the idea of anyone having to pretend to be something that they are not, just to be able to eat or feed their children. I refuse to let my people endure that horrible feeling that must somehow bear some semblance to what our Ancestors endured. If there is *ANYTHING* that we can do to help any of you, *KNOW* that we are *HERE*. And we *SEE* you.

Chapter 2- The Basics, Witches

This Chapter will be about basic knowledge that Witches need in order to get the 'Crystal' Ball rolling. It will not delve into everything, but just some of the Basics to get you started. As previously stated, this is not based on any particular Path- but the resources are drawn from many places that I have tapped into over the years. It is basically the way our Coven, The Silver Moon Society Coven does things and some of the basics we teach new seekers before they are fully Initiated.

The Wiccan Rede

One of the first things you need to know is the Wiccan Rede. It is basically like our version of the Ten Commandments of The Christian Faith, but a little less vengeful and more chill. Especially regarding the whole bossiness of the 'Thall shall nots'. It's more like guidelines and common sense. In saying this, not everyone in our Coven considers themselves Wiccan. Some consider themselves to be in the 'Pagan' category, as that is a more general term that encompasses many different forms of Witchcraft. We all choose to abide by the Wiccan Rede, because it just seems to fit, as I said. More like Common Sense.

The Full Version of The Wiccan Rede is as follows:

Bide the Wiccan Laws we must In Perfect Love and Perfect Trust.
Live and let live. Fairly take and fairly give.
Cast the Circle thrice about to keep the evil spirits out.
To bind the spell every time let the spell be spake in rhyme.
Soft of eye and light of touch, Speak little, listen much.
Deosil go by the waxing moon, chanting out the Witches' Rune.
Widdershins go by the waning moon, chanting out the baneful rune.
When the Lady's moon is new, kiss the hand to her, times two.
When the moon rides at her peak, then your heart's desire seek.

Heed the North wind's mighty gale, lock the door and drop the sail.
When the wind comes from the South, love will kiss thee on the
mouth.
When the wind blows from the West, departed souls will have no rest.

When the wind blows from the East, expect the new and set the feast.
Nine woods in the cauldron go, burn them fast and burn them slow.
Elder be the Lady's tree, burn it not or cursed you'll be.
When the Wheel begins to turn, let the Beltane fires burn. When
the Wheel has turned to Yule, light the log and the Horned One
rules.
Heed ye flower, Bush and Tree, by the Lady, blessed be.
Where the rippling waters go, cast a stone and truth you'll know.
When ye have a true need, hearken not to others' greed.
With a fool no season spend, lest ye be counted as his friend.
Merry meet and merry part, bright the cheeks and warm the heart.
Mind the Threefold Law you should, three times bad and three times
good.
When misfortune is enow, wear the blue star on thy brow.
True in love ever be, lest thy lover's false to thee. Eight
words the Wiccan Rede fulfill:

'An ye harm none, do what ye will'

The Pentacle

The next bit of useful information that Baby Witches need to know
is about the Pentacle and what it represents. The Pentacle is an
upright five-pointed star, enclosed in a circle. The Star represents
the four elements- Earth, Air, Fire and Water- and The Spirit. The
circle around the Star represents Protection. Protection from
negativity from 'The Goddess', or from whichever Deity that you
feel connected with. This is one of those 'A Rose by any other
name' things. I feel that The Goddess, The Great Spirit, The Creator,

The Universe, Gaia, God or whatever other name you use to label her/him/them... I feel they are all one in the same. (Just like I personally feel that most religions originate from Ancient Paganism in some degree) Some people will disagree with me on that, but I feel this to be the way things are and that is basically how our Coven observes this.

The Wheel of The Year

The Wheel of The Year represents the Eight Pagan Sabbats. These are the Eight Major Holidays that are usually lined up with Christian Holidays (Early Christian leaders felt it would help to Convert Pagans by renaming Ancient Pagan Holidays and associating them with Christian beliefs.)

Here are the Correspondences:

Yule- Christmas

Imbolc- Groundhog Day

Ostara- Easter/ Spring Equinox

Beltane- May Day

Litha- Summer Solstice

Lughnassad/Lammas- Loaf Mass Day (a Harvest Festival)

Mabon- Autumnal Equinox

Samhain- Halloween/ All Souls Day/ Dios De La Muertos

Every Sabbat has its own correspondences associated with it. And every spoke on the Wheel of The Year tells a Story about the cycles of life and death of the God and Goddess. The Sabbats are the Eight *main*

Holidays, but each Full Moon is also Celebrated, and they are called Esbats.

The Full Moon- Esbats

Every Full Moon has a Name, and it is usually based on the season or something that associated with that time of year. Here is a list of The Traditional Wiccan Names of The Full Moons:

January ~ Cold Moon

February ~ Quickening Moon

March ~ Storm Moon

April ~ Wind Moon

May ~ Flower Moon

June ~ Sun Moon

July ~ Blessing Moon

August ~ Corn Moon

September ~ Harvest Moon

October ~ Blood Moon

November ~ Mourning Moon

December ~ Long Nights Moon

The Moon's phases can directly affect the outcome of Spellcasting. The Full Moon is usually good for bringing something to you, like if you wanted make your Herb Garden grow better and wanted to use Magick to help- you'd do an abundance Spell or a Fertility Spell, to bring those characteristics into your life. That type of Spell would be best performed on a Full Moon. But a New Moon is best for doing Spells to rid something for your life. Banishing Spells, to rid your life of negativity are best done on the New Moon, or the Dark Moon.

The phases in between can be used to your advantage too. Usually the Waxing Moon is like the Full Moon and can manifest, and the Waning Moon is like the New Moon or Dark Moon, useful for banishing

Common Correspondences For Magickal Purposes

In Magick, symbolism is particularly important. Like manifests *Like*. The Colors have important meanings when drafting and casting Spells. Here are Some Color Properties to consider the next time you dress for success:

Color Correspondences

White - Attracting, Purifying, Cleansing, Protection, Balancing, Clarity, Divination, Grounding, Guidance, Healing, Higher Self, Hope, Innocence, Optimism, Peace, Spirituality, Truth, Will Power and Workplace Magic.

White is also thought of as an all-purpose candle. White candles can generally be used to replace other colors when they are not available.

Black - Absorbing, Acceptance, Anger, The Afterlife, Banishing, Binding, Challenges, Determination, Death, Endings, Justice, Loss, Release, Break Hexes, Security, Grief, Negativity, Magic, Patience, Persistence, Rebirth, Karma, Secrets, Spirituality, Strength and Self Control.

Red - Courage, Assertiveness, Business, Creativity, Energy, Desire, Love, Loyalty, Motivation, Passion, Romance, Strength, Power, Action, Survival, Change and Overcoming obstacles.

Yellow - Action, Communication, Friendships, Learning new skills, Loans and Credit, Business, Happiness, Intellect, Inspiration, Intuition, Knowledge, Wisdom, Pleasure, Stimulation and Travel.

Pink - Acceptance, Affection, Beauty, Compassion, Reconciliation, Children, Healing Abuse, Fidelity, Family, Friendship, Femininity, Kindness, Love, Marriage, Nurturing, Passion, Sensuality and Love.

Green - Abundance, Acceptance, Action, Agriculture, Beauty, Change, Creativity, Family, Fertility, Harmony, Healing, Luck, Longevity, Environment, Nurturing, Partnerships, Peace and Prosperity.

Purple - Astrology, Authority, Enlightenment, Spiritual Development, Psychic Protection, Emotions, Imagination, Influence, Independence, Power, Spirituality, Truth, Wisdom, Writing, Addiction and Overcoming Fears.

Orange - Abundance, Adaptability, Ambition, Celebration, Confidence, Creativity, Courage, Discipline, Vitality (Energy), Independence, Freedom, Goals, Justice, Money, Positivity, Pleasure, Reconciliation, Stimulation, Strength and Travel.

Blue - Honesty, Trust, Communication, Dreamwork, Sleep, Mental obstacles, Wisdom, Pregnancy, Leadership, Justice, Career, Marriage, Interviews and Study.

Brown - Material matters, Endurance, Hard Work, Animals, Balance, Courage, Grounding, Finding lost objects, Stability, Material Protection.

Silver - Awareness, Healing, Intuition, Divination, Money, Psychic Powers, Purification, Hidden Potential, Fertility, Feminine Energy, Stability, Success, Sea, Moon and Star Magic and The Goddess.

Gold - Abundance, Fame and Fortune, Ambitions, Money, Positivity, Happiness, Creativity, Divination, Power, Influence, Luxury, Masculine Energy, Sun Magick and The God.

Days of the Week have importance, as do times of Day when drafting Spells. The Days of The Week Magickal Properties are as Follows:

Sunday Magickal Correspondences

Planet: Sun

Element: Fire

Gender: Masculine

Deities: Apollo, Brigid, Helios, Ra

Colors: Amber, Gold, Orange Yellow

Crystals: Amber, Diamonds, Carnelian, Gold, Quartz Sunstone, Tiger's Eye, Yellow Topaz

Herbs & Plants: Angelica, Buttercups, Cinnamon, Eyebright, Juniper, Marigolds, St. John's Wort, Sunflowers

Incenses: Cedar, Cinnamon Frankincense, Lemon, Sun Oil

Energies & Associations: Agriculture, Beauty, Creativity, Ego, Fame, Fatherly Love, God Rituals, Hope, Male Health, Personal Achievements, Power, Promotions, Self-Expression, Spiritual Connection, Success, Victory, Wealth

Extras: Sunday sets the tone for the rest of the week; ensure that Sundays are full of light, fun, and happiness.

Monday Magickal Correspondences

Planet: Moon

Element: Water

Gender: Feminine

Deities: Artemis, Diana, Luna, Selene, Thoth

Colors: Silver, White, Gray, Blue

Crystals: Aquamarine, Moonstone, Mother-of-Pearl, Opal, Pearl, Quartz, Sapphire, Selenite, Silver

Herbs & Plants: Catnip, Chamomile, Comfrey, Lily, Lotus, Mints,

Moonflowers, Moonwort, Myrrh, Poppy, Sage, Sandalwood, Willow

Incenses: Honeysuckle, Jasmine, Moon Oil, Sandalwood, Wormwood

Energies & Associations: Clairvoyance, Divination, Dream Work, Emotional Healing, Faerie Magick, Feminine Beauty, Female Fertility, Feminine Health, Glamour, Goddess Rituals, Home and Family Life, Illusions, Intuition, Insight, Psychic Ability, Purity, Wisdom, Women's Mysteries

Tuesday Magickal Correspondences

Planet: Mars

Element: Fire

Gender: Masculine

Deities: Ares/Aries, Lilith Mars, The Morrigan, Tiwaz, Tyr

Colors: Red, Black, Orange

Crystals: Bloodstone, Flint, Garnet, Iron Pink Tourmaline, Red Jasper, Red Tourmaline, Rhodonite, Ruby, Steel

Herbs & Plants: Allspice, Basil, Cactus, Chili Pepper, Coneflower, Dragon's Blood, Garlic, Ginger, Holly, Horseradish, Mustard, Stinging Nettle, Onion, Pepper, Pine, Radish, Thistles, Tobacco

Incenses: Basil, Black Pepper, Dragon's Blood, Ginger, Patchouli

Energies & Associations: Aggression, Breaking Negative Spells, Competition Courage, Defense, Dominance, Ego, Force, Hunting, Initiation, Leadership, Lust, Masculine Marriage and Protection, Powerful Protection, Powerful Wards, Revenge, Romance, Sex, Strength, Success, Victory, War and Conflict

Wednesday Magickal Correspondences

Planet: Mercury

Element: Air

Gender: Masculine

Deities: Athena, Hermes, Lugh, Mercury, Odin, Woden

Colors: Yellow, Silver, Gray, Purple, Orange, Mixed Colors Crystals: Agates, Amber, Aventurine, Citrine, Lapis Lazuli, Mercury/Quicksilver, Pumice, Sodalite, Zinc

Herbs & Plants: Aspen Trees, Ferns, Lavender, Lilies, Periwinkle

Incenses: Eucalyptus, Mercury Oil, Jasmine, Lavender, Sweetpea

Energies & Associations: Answers, Arts, Business Transaction, Chance, Charisma, Communication, Creativity, Debt, Divination, Education, Fear, Flexibility, Fortune, Gambling, Luck, Mental Health, Psychic Work, Quickness, Study, Summoning Spirits, Swiftness, Teaching, Travel, Work, Writing

Thursday Magickal Correspondences

Planet: Jupiter

Element: Earth

Gender: Masculine

Deities: Juno, Jupiter, Thor, Zeus

Colors: Blue, Green, Purple, Rich Royal Colors

Crystals: Aventurine, Amethyst, Brown Jasper, Green Lodestone, Green Tourmaline, Lapis Lazuli, Malachite, Peridot, Tin, Turquoise

Herbs & Plants: Anise, Borage, Cinquefoil, Clove, Dandelion, Dill, Fig, Honeysuckle, Hyssop, Maple, Meadowsweet, Mint, Nutmeg, Oak, Patchouli, Sage, Star Anise

Incenses: Cinnamon, Clove, Jupiter Oil, Musk, Nutmeg, Oakmoss, Patchouli, Sage

Energies & Associations: Abundance, Career, Employment,

Energetic Increase, Expansion, Generosity, Growth, Happiness, Healing, Harvesting, Honest Leadership, Honor, Leadership, Legal Matters, Loyalty, Luck, Male Fertility, Material Opportunities, Money, Optimism, Power, Prosperity, Protection, Riches, Wealth

Friday Magickal Correspondences

Planet: Venus

Element: Water

Gender: Female

Deities: Aphrodite, Eros, Freya, Venus

Colors: Aqua, Copper Colors, Green, Light Blue, Pink

Crystals: Aventurine, Blue Lace Agate, Copper, Coral, Emerald, Jade, Lapis Lazuli, Malachite, Moonstone, Quartz, Rose Quartz, Selenite

Herbs & Plants: African Violet, Apples, Apple blossoms, Apricot, Barley, Birch, Cardamom, Carnations, Catnip, Columbine, Feverfew, Foxglove, Germanium, Goldenrod, Heather, Hibiscus, Iris, Lilac, Magnolia, Roses, Strawberries, Sweetpea, Thyme

Incenses: Cardamom, Rose, Saffron, Sandalwood, Strawberry, Vanilla, Venus Oil, Yarrow

Energies & Associations: Arts, Beauty, Birth, Fertility, Friendship, Growth, Harmony, Love, Marriage, Music, Nature, Partnerships, Peace, Perfumes, Platonic Love, Lust, Passion, Pleasure, Reconciliation, Relationships, Resolving Relationship Issues, Romance, Sexuality, Social Activities, Transformation

Saturday Magickal Correspondences

Planet: Saturn

Element: Earth, Fire

Gender: Female

Deities: Cronos, Fates, Hecate, Loki, Saturn,

Colors: Purple, Black, Maroon, Dark Colors, Indigo

Crystals: Apache Tear, Black Onyx, Coal, Coral, Hematite, Jet, Lead, Obsidian, Pewter, Salt, Serpentine, Smoky Quartz, Tourmaline,

Herbs & Plants: Amaranth, Beet, Belladonna, Boneset, Comfrey, Cypress, Hellebore, Hemlock, Hemp, Ivy, Mimosa, Morning Glory, Mullein, Quince, Skullcap, Slippery Elm, Thyme

Incenses: Cypress, Myrrh, Patchouli, Saturn Oil

Energies & Associations: Agriculture, Apprehension, Banishment, Binding, Boundaries, Caution, Cleansing, Creativity, Cursing, Destruction of All that Does Not Serve, Elderly Care, Endings, Exorcism, Fortune, Freedom, Hexing, Hidden Matters, Hope, Limitations, Locating Lost Items or People, Longevity, Meditation, Overcoming Obstacles, Protection, Psychic Defense, Revealing Truth, Self-Discipline, Spiritual Communication

Crystal Correspondences

These are some of the Magickal Properties of Crystals.

Agate: Dream magic, Wealth, Protection from Evil (especially Evil Eye), Vitality, Fertility

Amber: Peace and Harmony, Love, Meditation, Purification, Air Magic

Amethyst: Psychic Powers, Break Addictions, Divine Love, Meditation

Ametrine: Survival, Clarity and Strength of Will, Protection of Business

Apatite: Great remover of what is unwanted and unnecessary (especially guilt)

Aquamarine: Hope, Psychic Abilities, Prevent from Seduction, Water Magic

Aventurine: Earth Magic, Stability, Money and Financial Magic

Anandalite: Cosmic Knowledge, Akashic Records, Connection of all Things

Bloodstone Perseverance, Vitality, Fire Magic

Calcite: Opens Spiritual Doors, additional Properties are depending on color

Carnelian: Magical and Psychic power Booster, Dispels Shyness and Self-Doubt

Cat's Eye: Clairvoyance, Confidence, Familiars (especially cats)

Celestite: Healing Magic, Relaxation, Sleep, Dream Magic
Chalcedony Joys of Life, Dispel Depression

Chrysocolla: Self-Love Magic, Expression, Magic for Serenity and Peace

Chrysolite: Magic for Wealth especially associated with Fame

Chrysoprase: Friendship Magic, Connection with Guides and Nature Spirits/Elementals

Citrine: Money and Financial Magic, Abundance, Energizing and Revitalizing Magic, Air Magick

Coral: (not a crystal) Love Magic, Emotional Healing Magic, Reveal Secrets, Friendship, Sea and Water Magic

Diamond: Prophecy, Channeling, Healing Magic, Money Magic, Magical Catalyst

Emerald: Wish fulfilment, Joy and Love Spells, Wealth, Good Luck Spells, Akashic Records and Past Lives

Fluorite: Creativity and Mental Powers, Healing Magic, Reverse Bad Luck, Prophetic Dreams, Air Magic

Garnet: Sex Magic, Magical Regeneration, Fertility and Vigor, Fire Magic

Hematite: Purification, Fertility for Women, Realization, Manifestation, Protection, Fire Magic

Jade: Immortality and Vitality, Divine blessings, Money Magic, Success Spells

Jasper: Weather Magic, Wish Spells- more depends on the color

Kyanite: Water Magic, Emotional Healing Magic, Freedom, Speech and Creativity

Labradorite: Psychic Powers, Transformation, Instill and Endure Change, Wisdom

Lapis Lazuli: Beauty Spells, Love Spells, Psychic Protection, Clarity and Peace

Malachite: Wisdom, Natural Magic, Protects against the Evil Eye, Attract Lover Spells, Communication with Magical/Spiritual Entities

Moonstone: Love, Divination, Prophecy, Wisdom, Beauty, Water Magic

Obsidian: Grounding, Divination, Meditation, Alluring and Charming Spells, Summoning Spirits, Lighting Magic

Onyx: Summoning Spirits, Protection, Absorbing Negativity, Grounding, Earth Magic, Astral Projection, Spells for Karma and Spiritual Time Travelling

Opal: Reveal the Truth, Clairvoyance, Success

Pearl: Water Magic, Love and Beauty Spells, Stores Magical Spells

Peridot: Emotional Healing Magic (especially Jealousy), Money and Abundance Spells, Fame, Inner Strength

Quartz: Divine Love, Magic Amplifier, Magic Storage, Remove Energy Blockages

Rhodochrosite: Love Issues, Self-Love, Compassion, Identify Problems

Rhodonite: Inspiration, Love Spells (especially attracting soulmates), Confidence, Self-Worth

Rose Quartz (Pink Quartz): Friendship and Love Spells, Beauty Spells, Peace and Tranquility

Ruby: Sex and Love Spells, Health and Vitality Spells, Psychic and Magical Abilities, Protection from Sorcery

Sapphire: Creation, Fertility Magic, Love and Beauty Spells, Protection from all Harm

Selenite: Connection with Positive Magical/Spiritual Entities, Wisdom, Peace, Spiritual Guidance, Radiance

Sodalite: Water Magic, Fairy Magic, Courage, Protection, Dream Magic

Staurolite: Protection, Fairy Magic, Good Luck, Optimism

Shungite: Clairvoyance, Visions, Hidden Knowledge, Connection with Spirits

Topaz: Mystical Power, Wealth, Protection, Radiance (depends on color)

Tourmaline: Attraction, Wealth and Power, Spirit Magic, Occult Wisdom (depends on color)

Turquoise: Protection from Evil Eye, Healing Magic, Water Magic, Calm and Peace

Unakite Balance, Creativity, Love and Sex Magic, Passion for Life

Herbal Witchery (Kitchen Witchin')

Herbs can be prepared in numerous ways and each have their own Magickal and Medicinal Properties. You can make Teas, Brews, Poultices, Ointments, Tinctures and Incense to name a few. Here is a List of some Helpful Herbs for your Grimoire.

Success & Money	Healing	Creativity	Wisdom & Intellect	Balance & Harmony
Thyme	Caraway	Verbena	Bay	Chamomile
Basil	Mint	Jasmine	Rosemary	Sage
Ginger	Sage	Bay Leaves	Sage	Lavender
Cloves	Sandalwood	Angelica	Star/Anise	Ambergris
Nutmeg	Aloe	Ginseng	Almond	
Cinnamon	Saffron	Green Tea	Black Walnut	
Dill	Hemp			
Spirituality & Psychic Power	Protection	Grounding	Confidence	Sexual Love, Passion, Love, Energy
Calendula	Comfrey	Moss	Thyme	Ginger
Nutmeg	Mugwort	Sage	Mullen	Calendula
Bay	Sage	Turmeric	Sweet Pea	Marjoram
Thyme	Angelica	Sycamore	Yarrow	Mint
Sandalwood	Verbena	Lavender	Plumeria	Thyme
Celery	Mullen	Damiana	Black Walnut	Ginseng
Black Walnut	Ginseng	Dandelion	Rosemary	Jasmine
Mugwort	Cinnamon	Rosemary	Yarrow	Dill
	Lavender		Allspice	Chili Peppers
				Turmeric
Concentration	Purification	Removing Negative Energy	Intuition	Longevity
Caraway	Basil	Clove	Mugwort	Rose Hips
Vanilla	Cinnamon	Sage	Chamomile	Plumeria
Spearmint	Mint	Verbena	Rose buds	Sage
Savory	Parsley	Bamboo	Peppermint	Mugwort
Rosemary	Coconut	Coconut	Green Tea	

Deities: Goddesses

Amaterasu — Japanese sun Goddess

Annapurna — Hindu Goddess of Food and Nourishment

Aphrodite /Venus — Greek Goddess of love and beauty

Artemis/Diana — Greek/Roman Goddess of the hunt, virginity, and childbirth, twin sister of Apollo, and an Olympian, often associated with the moon

Astarte — Phoenician Goddess of fertility, sexuality, and war

Athena — Greek Goddess of wisdom, defensive and strategic wars

Bast — Egyptian solar and war Goddess (in the form of a cat)

Brigid — Celtic Goddess of poetry, healing, and crafts (especially smith-work), holy wells and eternal flames

Cerridwen — Celtic Goddess of transformation, of the cauldron of inspiration, of prophecy

Cybele — Greek Earth Mother

Danu — Irish Mother Goddess

Demeter — Greek Goddess of the harvest and of grain, mother of Persephone

Durga — Hindu Great Goddess, Divine Mother

Eos — Greek Goddess of the dawn

Ereshkigal — Mesopotamian Goddess of Darkness, Death, and Gloom

Flora — Roman Goddess of flowers

Fortuna — Roman Goddess of fortune

Freya or Freyja — Norse Goddess of fertility, sexual liberty, abundance, and war

Frigg — Norse Goddess of marriage, household management, and love, Queen of Heaven, and wife of Odin

Gaia/Earth Mother — The Greek Goddess Gaia is the primordial Goddess of earth, mother and grandmother of the first generation of Titans

Hathor — Egyptian Goddess of the Milky Way, Mother Goddess, Goddess of childbirth and death

Hecate — Greek Goddess of witchcraft and Magick, crossroads, and the harvest moon

Hestia — Greek Goddess of the hearth and domestic life

Hel — Norse Goddess daughter of Loki and the giantess Angrboda, Queen of the Dead

Hera — Roman Goddess of the Hearth, of women, and of marriage

Inanna — Sumerian Goddess of sexual love, fertility, and warfare

Isis — Egyptian Mother Goddess, matron of nature and Magick, Goddess of creativity and the underdog

Ishtar — Mesopotamian Goddess of sexual love, fertility, and war

Juno — Roman Queen of the Gods and Goddess of matrimony

Kali — Hindu Goddess of Time and Death, slayer of demons, protectress (As Kali Ma: Divine Mother Goddess)

Kore — Greek Maiden Goddess of bountiful Earth (See also Persephone)

Kwan Yin, Kwan Yin Ma, Quan Yin — Chinese Goddess of Mercy and Compassion

Lakshmi — Hindu Goddess of Wealth and Fertility (Goddess as Mother/Sustainer)

Lalita — Hindu Goddess of Beauty

Luna — Roman Goddess of the Moon

MA' at — Egyptian Goddess, personified concept of truth, balance, justice, and order

Mary — Mother Goddess, Queen of Heaven, Goddess of Femininity

Maya — Hindu Goddess of Illusion and Mystery

Minerva — Roman Goddess of wisdom and war

Morrigan — Celtic war Goddess

Nut — Egyptian Goddess of heaven and the sky and all celestial bodies

Parvati — Hindu Divine Mother, the embodiment of the total energy in the universe, Goddess of Power and Might

Pele — Hawai'ian volcano Goddess, Destroyer and Creatrix

Persephone — Greek Goddess daughter of Demeter, Queen of the Underworld, also a grain— Goddess, Maiden Goddess

Radha — Hindu Divine Mother

Rhiannon — Celtic Goddess of the moon

Rosmurta — Celtic/Roman Goddess of abundance. She is also the Goddess of Business Success.

Sarasvati — Hindu Goddess of Knowledge, the Arts, Mathematics, Education, and cosmic Wisdom (Creatrix)

Sedna — Inuit Goddess of the Sea and Queen of the Underworld

Selene — Greek Goddess of Moon

Shakti — Hindu primordial cosmic energy, Great Divine Mother

Shekinah — Hebrew Goddess of compassion in its purest form (feminine aspect of God)

Sita — Hindu Goddess representing perfect womanhood

Sol — Norse Sun Goddess

Sophia   Greek Goddess of wisdom

Spider Woman — Teotihuacan Great Goddess (Creatrix)

Tara — Hindu, Mother Goddess, the absolute, unquenchable hunger that propels all life.

Tara, Green — Buddhist female Buddha, Tibetan Buddhism - compassion, liberation, success. Compassionate Buddha of enlightened activity

Tara, White — Buddhist Goddess known for compassion, long life, healing and serenity; also known as The Wish— fulfilling Wheel, or Cintachakra

Tara, Red — fierceness, magnetizing all good things

Tara, Black — power

Tara, Yellow — wealth and prosperity

Tara, Blue — transmutation of anger

Tiamat — Mesopotamian dragon Goddess, embodiment of primordial chaos (the Velvet Dark)

Uma — Hindu Goddess of power, the personification of light and beauty, embodying great beauty and divine wisdom

Vesta — Roman Goddess of the hearth

Voluptas — Roman Goddess of pleasure

Yemaya — Yoruba Mother Goddess, Goddess of the Ocean White

Buffalo Calf Woman— Lakota Goddess

Gods

Adonis — Greek God of rebirth and vegetation, worshipped in mystery religions for untold eons

Apollo   Greek/Roman young solar God, God of light, truth and prophecy, God of archery, medicine and healing, God of music, poetry, and the arts

Anubis — Egyptian God of the Dead

Aten — Egyptian Supreme God, solar deity

Brahma — Hindu Creator God

Coyote — First Nations Trickster God

Cernunnos — Celtic God of the Wild Hunt, fertility and masculine energy

Dagda — Irish Father God, somewhat comical and bawdy

Dionysus — Greek/Roman God of wine, of ritual ecstasy, God of agriculture, music, and theatre, communication between living and dead

Eros — Greek God of sexuality and fertility

Ganesh — Hindu God with elephant head, remover of obstacles, God of beginnings, patron of arts and sciences, of intelligence and wisdom

Gopala — Hindu Child God, young Krishna, playful and mischievous while always aware of divinity

Govinda — Sikh God, preserver, protective father

Great Spirit — First Nations supreme Deity, Creator, Source

Hades — Greek God of the Underworld and Death

Hephaestus — Greek God of the Forge, of technology, craftsmen, sculptors, fire and volcanoes

Hermes — Greek God of boundaries and travelers, shepherds and cowherds, orators, writers and poets, invention, commerce, and thieves. Messenger of the Gods. Trickster God.

Herne — British God of vegetation, vine, and the wild hunt

Holly King — English God of winter (rest, withdrawal)

Horus — Egyptian Sky God, God of sun and moon, God of war and the hunt

Krishna — Hindu Supreme God, essence of all creation

Loki — Norse Trickster God, shapeshifter and gender-changer

Lugh — Celtic Sun God, God of smiths and artisans, harvest god

Mercury — Roman God of commerce, messenger of the Gods, speed and travel.

Mithras — Persian God of light

Oak King — English God of summer (expansion, growth, activity)

Odin — Norse Father God, God of wisdom, wealth, inspiration, poetry, battle, hunting, Magick, prophecy

Osiris — Egyptian God of the Underworld and the harvest

Pan — Greek nature God, Horned God, god of shepherds and flocks, of wild forests and fields, virility, fertility and spring

Ra — Egyptian God, solar deity

Rama — Hindu God representing the perfect human man and husband

Set / Seth — Egyptian God of chaos, war, storms, desert

Shiva — Hindu God, the destroyer of obstacles, transformer

Sunna — Norse Sun God

Tammuz — Egyptian green God

Thoth — Egyptian God of Magick and wisdom

Vishnu — Hindu God, sustainer

Zeus — Father God, Sky God

The Altar and Craft Tools

Altar Set-up varies for most Individuals, but Almost all Witches prefer to set one up, as it makes it easier to perform your rituals and to include your Altar in your Sacred Space when you cast your Circle. Usually facing the North in our Tradition, The Altar is very useful in that it gives you place to put the items you will use for your rituals, a place to put little representations of your Deities or Figurines, and the representations of the Elements. The Elements are usually represented with a Dish, Chalice or Goblet of water to represent the Element Water, A Dish of Sand, Salt or a Plant to represent Earth, A Lit Candle to Represent Fire and An Incense or Feather to Represent Air. Also, If you have other Tools that you'd like to use, This would be the place to put them as well. I usually have all of the above, along with Crystals, an Altar Pentacle, My Athame (Dagger), My Wand and My Book Of Shadows. I usually use a table for all of this because I am a notorious Hoarder and like to have everything that I need handy while doing my rituals.

Spells

The Last Chapter is the one you have suffered through this whole book for. Spells and Magickal Rituals. In This Chapter I will List Some Spells that I have stumbled upon over the past 25 years and some that I have drafted myself. I will also outline how you can also draft your very own personal and unique spells that will fit your needs exactly how you need them to. Once you get the hang of it, it's really a piece of cake! Always remember to cast your circle first and to protect yourself. You can protect yourself by anointing yourself in Ritual Oil or taking a Ceremonial Bath before rituals. My favorite and the easiest method to me, is to light a sage bundle and fan the smoke all over yourself and your sacred space. This is known as Smudging and is popular among American Indigenous Tribes. Use words of Affirmation to tell the negative vibes to respectively F#@* Off.

Simple Potato Love Spell

This Spell will require: a raw potato, split in

half

Some Rose Petals

2 Cinnamon sticks

Some Pink or Red Ribbon

Some Hair or Nail Clippings from you and your Lover (or a picture of you both)

Paper and Pen

Sandwich between the potato halves these items- Rose petals, cinnamon sticks, the hair, nails or pictures. On the Paper It should be about the size of a Post-it, write your desire- whether it's to reconnect, strengthen your bond, or encourage fidelity. Fold the paper until it's about the size of a quarter and put it in the middle of the potato halves. Firmly hold the potato together, and visualize your goal happening- imagine how you'll feel, what sensations your body will feel, sense, smell and taste. Think on this for at least five minutes. When you are satisfied with you visualization, wrap the potato with the ribbon. Say These Words while you do:

'Your Love is True and So is Mine,

And May we never Part.

As this plant grows, so does our Bond

You'll never break my Heart.

I am yours, and you belong to me,

As I will it, so shall it be.'

Plant The Potato in your yard or in a big flower pot and tend it well. As the plant grows, so will your bond.

A Simple Come To Me Spell You

will only need these items:

A Taper Candle

A Straight Pin or Safety Pin

It usually helps to dress the candle any time you use on in Magick, but if you do not have anointing oil, regular olive oil will work just fine. To dress the candle, you will carve your target's name into the candle from top to bottom three times with the pin. Then you will sprinkle some oil on your hands and rub from the top to the bottom of the candle until it is not complexly saturated in oil, but a little glossy and shiny. Try not to get it on the wick, as you do not want a towering inferno on your altar. At least not for this spell.

You will then hold the candle and whisper to it these words:

'It is not the candle that I mean to stick,

but_____'s heart that I mean to prick.

I call to you now, _____ Come to me,

As I will it, so Shall it Be.'

Stick the pin into the side of the candle a little way down from the top along the side. By the time it burns down, if your intentions are pure, they will turn up by the time the candle burns down to the pin.

Simple Money Spell This

Spell will require:

A Green Votive or Spell Candle

A Dollar Bill

A Quarter

A Dime

A Nickle

A Penny

Some Green Rice Offering or any Other Appropriate Offering

This I learned years ago. It is a 'Gypsy' Romany Spell for Money.

Dress your candle with oil after carving your needed amount of money onto it with a stick pin or your Athame. Anoint The Money with the oil, just wet your finger with the oil and touch each piece of money and visualize the blessings coming to you as you do this. Sit the Dollar down on your Altar and place the candle on top of it. Place the Coins at the 4 Cardinal directions around the candle. Light the candle.

Repeat These Words Three, Times Three.

(Say it 3 times in a row, then three more, then three more for a total of nine times.

'Trinka- Five.'

Meditate on why you need the money and see your financial problems vanishing in your mind's eye until the candle burns out.

When the Spell is done and the wax has cooled, bury the candle remnants on your property close to your front door. This will draw the Prosperity to you. The Spell was done and blessed for money, and imbibed with that energy, so the remnants being by your door will pull more money energy to you. (Like, attracts *Like*)

Past Life Dreaming Spell

Take a Ritual Cleansing Bath with Lavender Oil and Purple Candles Lit. After your bath, drink a warm cup of Chamomile Tea. Dress for bed, turn off your ringtone and try to make it so that nothing can disturb your sleep.

Lay in bed on your back and repeat the words:

'Remove the Chains of Time and Space

And make my Spirit soar- Make

these Mortal Arms embrace the

Life that was Before.'

Repeat it Twice more, slower and slower. Breathe slowly and listen to and feel your heartbeat.

Clear your mind. Feel your body relax slowly, melting into the soft cushioning of the mattress. Now try to remember your last birthday. All the details you can remember. Fell the sensations you felt that day.

Then the Previous Birthday. Where were you? What were you doing?

And Then the next Birthday.

Repeat until you get all the way back to when you were a young child. Do not anything distract you as you keep regressing further and further into your memories of your birthdays. Keep going and if there are some things that you can not actively remember, let your mind fill in the blanks. Sometimes your mind holds onto things deep in the recesses that we cannot remember right off. Now go back to when you were a baby, being held and fed. Keep going further back, and envision what childbirth must have felt like, and all of the sensations of seeing light and breathing air into you're your little lungs must have felt for the first time. Now go further, until you are inside, before birth- floating in the warm, safety of your Mother's Womb. Hear her Heartbeat and your own. Keep going backwards in time. Until your mind starts to receive images that may seem strange to you, places you have never been in this lifetime, faces of people you have never met. Take in all that you can until you finally fall asleep.

Dream...

When you wake up, before your get out of the bed, write down any and everything that you can remember. Try to be thorough. Once you stand up your memories will fade as the blood leaves your head and goes to the rest of your body. The images you saw and the sensations that you felt in your dream were distant memories of another lifetime. But also remember this: The mind can play tricks or get things jumbled up sometimes when it goes into overdrive by digging into places you usually don't go to. You may only have fragments and pieces. With practice and patience, it will become much easier to do this and to tell the difference between what real memories are and what are your mind's fabrications. But never use hard sedatives for this self-hypnosis technique. That would most assuredly cloud the truth from your mind, and it isn't healthy to build up an unnecessary dependence.

Quick and Easy Spells

These are little tricks that I found that I had written in my Old Book of Shadows from 15 or more years ago. Most of these I found in old tomes and books of voodoo and I think even from a collection of Medieval Spells that I once had access to.

- Anoint All your Cash with Magnet Oil prior to spending it so that it returns to you.
- A simple spell to bring money when you need it, burn onion peelings and skins on the stove. This will also drive off Evil.
- Burn Garlic skins in the kitchen to keep money in the house.
- Put Aspen Leaves and a Buckeye (Horse Chestnut) in a mojo bag and keep with you for luck and money.
- Put a Cinnamon Stick, green offering rice and 5 coins in a Conjure Bag. This will attract wealth to you.
- Carry or wear Tourmaline to attract cash.
- Bury an Acorn on the night of a Dark Moon in your yard to receive an infusion of cash.
- Sprinkle gold magnetic sand over a pair of lodestones (Natural magnets) and put in a red flannel piece of fabric with a dollar bill and a piece of fool's gold (Pyrite). This is a Gris Gris and will draw wealth.

Banishing Spells

- *Banishing Powder Recipe*- Black Pepper, Cayenne, Cinnamon, Sea Salt, and Sulfur blended in a mortar and pestle, stirred in a counterclockwise direction. Best made on a Dark Moon or New Moon.
- *Exodus Powder Recipe*- Asafetida, cayenne powder, sulfur (Add Black Salt and Graveyard Dirt to make Hot Foot Powder) Both are concentrated Banishing powders that can be sprinkled to keep someone away. Usually in their footprints or used in conjunction with a banishing spell with personal items of theirs.
- *Coffee Grounds Banishing Spell*- Gather dirt from your intended target's footprints or from under a chair that they've sat in. Combine it with cayenne powder, ground sassafras and used coffee grounds. Sprinkle the Mixture on their doorstep.
- *Four Thieves Banishing Spell for Debt Collectors*- Place their business card inside of a shot glass. Fill the glass with Four Thieves Vinegar. Leave the glass standing in a discreet spot for as long as necessary. *If a Business Card doesn't exist, make one up with their information (name, number, job title) on a 2x3 inch piece of paper) This will work just fine.
- *Garlic Banishing Spell*- Hang a Braid of 12 heads of Garlic on a nail above your front door to keep jealous people and The Evil Eye away.
- *Bean Rattle Banishing Spell*- Fill Dried Gourds or Rattles with dried beans. Shake them to drive away low-level Entities. Incorporate them into protection Spells. Spirits and Demons are said to be annoyed by the sound and they are said to leave.
- *Magick Mirror Demonic Banishment*- on a bright and sunny day, walk slowly around the infested area holding a

small round mirror, making sure to capture every area's reflection. Once you're done, hold the mirror face down and wrap in dark cloth. Immediately take it outside and very suddenly uncover it and hold it up toward the sunlight for no more and less than 9 seconds. Captured Malevolence and Negativity are rapidly burned out and destroyed. Place protective amulets in the now Demon-free area. You, the mirror and the area now require a heavy-duty spiritual cleansing. (This technique is derived from a ancient Chinese Tradition and has been recorded as being highly effective)

- *Mandrake Banishing Spells*- Place a Mandrake Root in a Room in a dark and hidden place to drive evil spirits away.
- *Poltergeist Door Slamming*- Slamming every door in your house three times is said to scare away poltergeists.
- *Sage Burning Ritual Banishing*- Burning Bundles of dried White Sage (Called Smudge Sticks or Sage Bundles) is known by many traditions among American Native Tribes to rid an area of evil spirits and negative energy.
- *Sinistrari's Demon Banishing Advice*- Ludovico Sinistrari was a 17th Century Franciscan Friar, Scholar and Demonologist. His method included these ingredients: Castor Oil, Coral, Jasper and Jet with Menstrual Blood. (Not exactly sure how this recipe was applied, but still thought it was interesting enough to mention in this book)
- *Trapped in a Bottle Banishment*- Evil Spirits, including Djinn can be trapped in vessels like Bottles or Jars. Drop 13 Rose thorns in a Jar, one by one. As you drop each on in, tell the Evil Presence to Leave, that it isn't welcome. Cover the Thorns with the petals from 1 Rose, dropping them in one at a time, repeating the spell. Fill the vessel 2/3 of the way up with salt water, holy water, rose of Jericho water, or Notre Dame water. Leave the jar open and unattended overnight in the affected area. Before sunrise,

close the jar tight. The evil should be trapped inside. Wrap the jar in dark fabric and bury it far away.
- *Witch Balls*- Globes of iridescent colored glass. Place them around your home to repel undesired Spirits. Speak your desire for them to leave.

Love Charms and Conjures

- *To Attract Women*- Wear Amethyst.

- *Bae-Bay Wish*- Write a tiny Love wish on a Bay Leaf with Lemon Juice. (Invisible Ink) Keep it in an Envelope.

- *Mead*- Mead, which is a beverage made from fermented honey is said to make love spells much more potent. Mead is one the most ancient intoxicant beverages that is still drank today and is rapidly regaining popularity.

- *Binding Love Leash Spell*- Following Sex, retain a cloth that was used to clean both partners. Tie seven knots around it. Place a rock inside big enough to weigh it down in water and tie a knot to secure it inside the cloth. Drop it in the River and plead with the River Spirit to Protect your Love. Only the maker of this charm can undo it by retrieving the charm from the river.

- *Happy Marriage Rosemary Spell*- A Newly wedded couple should dip a wand made from s thick sprig of Rosemary into their first drink and stir it as a married couple to ensure a Happy Marriage.

- *To remedy Marital Problems*- To help resolve issues in a Marriage, fill a glass with Holy water and sprinkle sea salt into it. Drop your wedding ring into it and let it soak overnight. As it does, remember your wedding vows and what they stood for.

- *Fidelity Hoodoo Spell-* One method of ensuring your husband's fidelity is to put menstrual blood in his food. (I do not advise this. It's pretty gross.)

Protection Magick

- *Evil Eye Removal Spell with An Egg-* This method is popular in Santeria and Romany (Gypsy) Cultures and is said to highly effective. It works best with fresh laid eggs. Have the person sit or lay in a comfortable position. Take

  one egg and pass it all over their person's body- going over their face, neck, heart, stomach, groin area, legs and then back up and around their outline where their Aura is. Do this three times, saying blessings of defiance against evil. With a blessed white candle lit, crack the egg into a bowl and look for any sign of blood. Dispose of it far away from the home. If signs of blood were present, further action should be taken.
- *Sending Back the Evil Eye Spell-* Sometimes you can sense Evil Eye right away, it can be neutralized immediately with this remarkably simple ritual from Egypt. As the person walks away, pick up and handful of dirt and toss it in their wake.
- *Burying A Garlic Bulb at each corner of your house will keep evil at bay.*
- *Brick Dust, Sea Salt or powdered Terracotta can be spread across your door way and windows to keep people who mean you harm away.*
- *For a Witch's Bottle Fill a bottle with nails, broken glass, your own hair or nail clippings, vinegar or your own urine and other protective herbs and ingredients. Seal it up and keep it in a safe dark place to protect yourself for dark*

intentions. Making one against an enemy can also be done with the right ingredients, for protection of course. This type should be buried.

<u>Old School Magick and Remedies</u>

(I wouldn't Try most of these if I were you. You decide which ones.)

- *A remedy for 'Madness' (Insanity) is to blend mild honey and salt and drink it from a sea shell before sunrise.*
- *For Dysentery crack a fresh egg and put the yoke into a glass of brandy and drink it.*
- *To Cure Hysteria take dried chicken manure and grind it up. Place it inside of a prune and feed it to the patient. (1691 London- An Actual Recipe)*
- *For Asthma- Boil Garlic in water and make it into a syrup with fresh honey.*
- *To Free yourself from a Love Spell 'make a Jakes' (My Son in Law is gonna love THAT) Meaning urinate or defecate into the Bewitcher's Shoe. (1655- London)*
- *Boil cedar leave in water. Wet your hands in it and 'strike' (I took this Bitch Slap) the Enchanter to free yourself from an Enchantment.*
- *To make someone afraid suspend a doll in their likeness from a string. (I would imagine seeing this would be damn creepy- so it is definitely effective)*
- *A 15th Century Charm to have a Loved one Fulfill a Promise- Boil a handful of daisies in a pint of water. Clean the roots of the same flowers. Boil for 5-30 minutes. Wish for the promise to come true during the whole process.*

When you have finished boiling, pour the contents over a dunghill. (A Pile of Poop)

On that note, I think we've had enough of these weird old spells. Now I think it is time to teach you how to do your own. Composing a Spell is not as hard as one would think. The main ingredient you need is intent. Set your intent, figure out what ingredients you need, assign properly corresponded colors, herbs, crystals, moon phase, day and time. After that the only thing left to do is write a nice little chant. Making it rhyme is not really a necessity, but the rhythm adds to the potency and makes it easier to remember. So let's break that down.

1. Set your intent. (Decide what you want and what you are willing to do to get it.)
2. Decide on the Proper Ingredients and Correspondences for your purpose.
3. Write a Little Ditty that'll get the Job done.

That's pretty much it. It does help to record all of your Magickal workings in your Book of Shadows, Grimoire or Journal (Whatever you call yours) The best way to get really good at Spell Crafting is to practice. Like I always say- Experience is the Best Teacher. Thanks For Reading. Blessed Be & Stay Fly, Witches!

~Raven Nightshade